HOW TO BE A TRUE FRIEND
The Bible Reveals Friendship's Heart

ISBN 978-1-949628-13-5
Printed in the United States of America.
10 9 8 7 6 5 4 3 2 1   22 21 20 19

Published by The Pastoral Center, http://pastoral.center.

Developed in partnership with MennoMedia and Brethren Press. Series editors: Fumiaki Tosu, Ann Naffziger, and Paul Canavese. *How to Be a True Friend*: Writer, Michele Hershberger. Project editor, Lani Wright. Staff editors, Susan E. Janzen, Julie Garber, and James Deaton. Updated design, Paul Stocksdale.

All rights reserved. Purchase of this book includes a license to reproduce this resource for use in a single parish, school, or other similar organization. You are allowed to share and make unlimited copies only for use within the organization that licensed it. If you serve more than one organization, each should purchase its own license. You may not post this document to any web site without explicit permission to do so. Outside of these conditions, no part of this book may be reproduced in any form or by any means, electronic or mechanical, including photocopying, recording, taping, or via any retrieval system, without the written permission of The Pastoral Center, 1212 Versailles Ave., Alameda, CA 94501. Thank you for cooperating with our honor system regarding our licenses.

For questions or to order additional copies or licenses, please call 1-844-727-8672 or visit http://pastoral.center.

Portions of this work © 2019 by The Pastoral Center / PastoralCenter.com. Adapted and published with permission from Generation Why Bible Studies. © 1997, 2015 Brethren Press, Elgin, IL 60120 and MennoMedia, Harrisonburg, VA 22803, U.S.A. All rights reserved.

Unless otherwise noted, the Scripture passages contained herein are from the *New Revised Standard Version of the Bible*, copyright © 1989 by the National Council of the Churches of Christ in the United States of America. Used by permission. All rights reserved.

>> Bible-based Explorations of Issues Facing Youth

>> OVERVIEW

When conversing online, the acronym IRL stands for "in real life." The virtual world of social media, text chats, blogs, and more have the power to remove us from the real world. What we experience online can skew our perspective on what it means to be human. It can numb us, incite us, distract us, depress us, confuse us, and make us rude or impatient. Strangely, this supposedly "social" and "connected" technology can profoundly disconnect us from others.

Religious faith can also place us in a bubble, especially when it distances us from others. When we keep the prophetic message at a safe distance, obscured in theological language and abstractions, we are missing the whole point. And when we see our parish as an insider club that serves itself, we can forget the radically inclusive message entrusted to us: God's love is for *everyone*, and God expects us to transform the *whole world* through that love.

Through the incarnation, God showed up in the real world to show us that our faith is not just about talking the talk, but also walking the walk. It can be risky. It can be confusing. It can hurt. But living out our faith can also bring us great purpose, peace, and joy.

This series connects the Bible with the tough questions that youth (and adults) encounter in their neighborhood, in school, among friends, and even online. This process will help you as a leader break open these issues in a fun and meaningful way, sparking conversation and the kind of life change Jesus invites us to embrace.

>> THE ROLE OF PARENTS

As children enter middle school and high school, they become more independent, self-reliant, and, well, self-centered. This can bring parents to make assumptions that this is the time to step back, giving their child more space to form their identity. While there is truth to that at some level (adolescents definitely shouldn't be smothered), this is a stage of life when parents should in fact *lean in*. The apparent confidence and bluster youth show on the outside can mask the insecurity and confusion on the inside. Youth need their parents to be involved more than ever.

>> WHOLE FAMILY FORMATION

Parents are the primary teachers of their own children, and parishes are waking up to the fact that faith formation programs need to bring parents into the process if they hope to see faith passed on to the next generation. Recent studies give us more and more evidence that the role of parents is the most important factor in determining whether a child will embrace faith as they move toward adulthood. Research from the Center for the Applied Research on the Apostolate shows that parents who talk about their faith and show through their actions that their faith is important to them are more likely to have children who remain Catholic.

More about Whole Family Formation >>>>

To learn more about how your parish can take a comprehensive whole family approach to faith formation, visit **GrowingUpCatholic.com**.

While whole family events with elementary-aged children are on the rise, the role of parents can be an afterthought in youth ministry. We have designed the sessions in this series to work with or without parents present, and we encourage you to offer them as parent-child events.

If you choose to involve parents, it is important to consider before each session how to best do so. Many of the activities in this series are high-energy, creative, or silly. Some parents may need some encouragement to get out of their heads and have fun with the group. A few activities involving physical contact would be inappropriate for parents and youth to participate together, and we have noted them as such.

There are a number of ways to approach discussions with parent participation. Unless you have a small group, you will likely want to break into smaller groups for conversation. Some youth may be self-conscious and unable to be completely honest and open in a group situation with a parent present. For this reason, you may choose in some cases to assign parents to different groups from their own children, or to have separate parent and child groups altogether. Be sure to cover expectations around confidentiality. It is inappropriate for a parent (or youth) to share with another parent what their child said in a small group.

Note that even if parents and their children do not share all conversations together in the session, they will still have a valuable shared experience and can have extended conversations about it later.

>> THANK YOU

The role you play in gathering, animating, praying with, and forming youth is a valuable one. Thank you for all you do to serve the church and its families!

Bible-based Explorations of Issues Facing Youth

»» HOW TO BE A TRUE FRIEND ««««
The Bible Reveals Friendship's Heart

»» INTRODUCTION

Why do the youth at your church dress alike?

Why won't they go to church camp unless their best friends go too?

Why do they all sit together at the back of the church? Are they joined at the hip?

They're friends. And if they're all sitting together, they're very normal. The real question is—are there any youth hanging on the edge waiting to sit there too?

Friendship is very important to youth. A peer group supplies much-needed security, loyalty, and love. With friends being so important to them, youth want to figure out what to look for, and how to make and keep friends.

Each session in this unit focuses on a quality that can raise relationships to a new level. Each quality is modeled by Bible figures—David and Jonathan (trust), Ruth and Naomi (loyalty), the Samaritan woman and Jesus (taking risks), Paul and Barnabas (reconciliation), and Jesus and his disciples (servanthood and commitment). All of the sessions address this question—what is a true friend?

This study has two additional goals. For one, this study hopes to encourage an intimate friendship with Jesus, the truest of friends. And second, most sessions (including the extender) incorporate smaller group settings where youth are encouraged to take off their masks—a level of vulnerability required for true and lasting friendship. Such sharing may be scary, but it's worth it.

Bathe the group in prayer. Expect a lot from them, and they'll give it to you. Ask questions. And have fun.

»
"There is nothing on this earth more to be prized than true friendship."

St. Thomas Aquinas

EXTENDER SESSION

Most units include one extender session, which includes suggestions for special activities related to the issue of the unit. Extender sessions help accommodate the diversity of parish schedules. Since each unit is undated, participants may study units in their entirety and still participate in special events of the parish that get scheduled simultaneously with youth group time. Extender sessions can be used anytime, but, depending on the option you choose, the one for this unit best follows **Session 3** or **Session 6**. Calculate now whether or not you will be using the extender session.

THE SESSION PLAN: The parts of the session guide

- **Faith story.** The session is rooted in this Bible passage.
- **Faith focus.** This is the story of the passage in a nutshell.
- **Session goal.** The entire session is built around this one goal. What changes—in knowledge, attitude, and/or action—do you desire in your group?
- **Materials needed and advance preparation.** This is what you will need if the session is to go smoothly. You'll feel more at ease if you've taken care of these details before you meet your group.

FROM LIFE TO BIBLE TO LIFE

The teaching plan is called *life-centered*. However, when we write each session, we always begin with scripture. We ask, what does this particular passage say, especially to youth? Each teaching session moves from life to Bible to life. So the Bible is indeed at the center of this way of teaching.

In every session we try to hit upon a tough question that participants might ask. Find out what questions on this issue are important for your group. Feel free to bring your own input and invite your group members to add their own experiences.

TEACHING THE SESSION

The five step-by-step movements will carry you from *life to the Bible and back to life*. Each session takes about 45 to 50 minutes. If there is a handout sheet for the session, take note of any complementary activities and stories.

1. **Focus.** Intended to create a friendly climate within the group and to *draw attention* to the issue.
2. **Connect.** Invites participants to *express* their own life experience about the issue, through talking, drawing, role playing, and other activities. Also uses memory, reason, or imagination to get the group thinking about *why* they view the issue the way they do.
3. **Explore the Bible.** What does the Bible *say* about the issue? With a minimum of lecturing, dig into the faith story and search for answers to questions raised in the first activities. The Insights from Scripture section will help clarify the faith story. Help participants discover how the faith community understands the Bible passage.
4. **Apply** the faith story. What does the Bible passage *mean* for contemporary life? This is the "aha!" moment when participants realize the faith story has wisdom for *their* lives.
5. **Respond.** Why does the Bible passage *matter*? What will the group do about the issue in light of what they have learned from their own experiences set alongside the faith story? How can we *live* the faith story rather than pass it off as a mere intellectual exercise?

LOOK AHEAD

Here are reminders for what you need to do for the next session or two.

INSIGHTS FROM SCRIPTURE

Here is a resource for Explore the Bible. Don't try to use all the material given. Take what you need to lead the session and answer questions your group may have. Let the Insights section inspire you to think and study more about the passage for the session.

›› HANDOUT SHEETS

Occasionally, there will be a handout sheet to complement your session. If you choose to use this, make enough copies for the group in advance of the session. These sheets may include questions, stories, agree/disagree exercises, charts, pictures, and other materials to stimulate thinking and discussion.

Generally, no participant preparation is required unless the session plan calls for you to contact selected group members for specific tasks.

>>> **SESSION 1**

TRUE FRIENDS CAN BE TRUSTED >>>

>>> KEY VERSE

Then Jonathan made a covenant with David, because he loved him as his own soul. (1 Samuel 18:3)

>>> FAITH STORY

1 Samuel 18:1-5; 20:1-42

>>> FAITH FOCUS

David and Jonathan were best friends. Jonathan was a son to King Saul, and David was the ever-growing threat to this king's popularity. When Saul threatened to kill David, Jonathan had to decide between family—his own right to the throne—and David. Jonathan proved to David his trustworthiness by making a covenant with him, creating a plan to warn him of danger, and by risking his own life for his friend.

>>> SESSION GOAL

Encourage participants to build trust in their friendships through consistent acts of kindness and by being reliable.

>>> Materials needed and advance preparation

- Blindfolds (*Option C* in Focus)
- Bibles
- Pencils/pens, writing paper
- Copies of the handout sheet for Session 1

TEACHING PLAN

1. FOCUS 6-10 minutes

>> **Option A: Safe Hands.** Gather the group and pair up. Each pair holds hands in lines facing each other. One participant then lies on the hands of the others. They try to raise that person in the air, lower to the ground, shake, roll from one side to the other, swing front to back, etc. The goal is that the single participant feels safe and secure even with all the movement. Encourage others to be carried before asking, *How did it feel to have to trust these people to hold and carry you?*

>> **Option B:** Trust Circle. Instruct the group to stand in a circle except for one volunteer who stands in the middle. (Make two circles if the group is too large to get close enough to catch the person falling.) The person in the middle stiffens her body, keeps feet together, and begins to fall, trusting the group to catch her. The group catches her and then gently pushes her to another part of the circle. The catch-and-push cycle continues for up to five times. Repeat the exercise until everyone has had the opportunity to be in the middle. Debrief by asking several of the participants how it felt when they were in the middle.

>> **Option C:** (if you have access to an outdoor area). Pair up, and blindfold one person in each pair. The sighted person must find ways to communicate with the partner in a way that builds trust, as they navigate either a wooded area or natural obstacles. Switch roles after 3-5 minutes. Debrief by asking what worked best to build trust, and what threatened trust. **Option:** Lead the partner through a forested area to a particular tree, and encourage the blindfolded one to get familiar with it, through touch, smell, and any sense other than sight. Then lead the blindfolded one back to the starting point, remove the blindfold, and have the person try to find the tree.

2. CONNECT 6-8 minutes

Have everyone sit in a circle, with backs to the center. Sitting on the floor may be easiest, but in chairs is fine too. Then say, *Think for a minute about these three questions:*

- *Whom do you trust in real life?*
- *Do your friends trust you? Why?*
- *What is the hardest trust issue you've had to face?*

Then invite anyone who is willing to turn toward the center of the circle and share their answer to *one* of the questions. After someone responds, they remain facing the center of the circle. Don't worry if there is a long silence, and don't be disappointed if no one shares. The experience may have been an intense one. Have everyone turn to the center of the circle when more than 30-45 seconds has passed since anyone shared.

3. EXPLORE THE BIBLE 8-10 minutes

Shift to this activity by saying: *It's important to know whom you can trust. There's a story of a guy named Jonathan who staked his whole future for his friend David.*

>> **Option A:** Have the group brainstorm all the facts they know about David and Jonathan. Fill in whatever pertinent details they leave out (see Insights from Scripture).

Then go to the scriptures, first 1 Samuel 18:1-5 and then all of chapter 20, asking them to look for ways Jonathan proved himself trustworthy. Challenge them to find seven things. (Answers might include: made a covenant, handed over his royal robe and armaments, promised to tell David of any plots on David's life, expressed his love for David, made a plan to save David's life, stood up for David even against his father Saul, was willing to give up his place on the throne, risked his life for David.) Have several volunteers read the passages, then ask these questions:

- *What is the significance of Jonathan giving away his sword and tunic and other things?*
- *In chapter 20, who does Jonathan trust at first—David or his father Saul? What did it take for Jonathan to catch on to what was really going on?*
- *What do you think angered Saul more and why—David's absence from the table or his own son's loyalty to David?*
- *Why did Jonathan risk death by going back home (v. 33)?*
- *Do you think Jonathan did the right thing to remain loyal to David? Did he betray his father?*

>>> **Option B:** View a video (or make and show one of your own!) that summarizes Jonathan and David's plan to save David's life, such as: https://youtu.be/qUzPlwmz_jw or https://youtu.be/pZ2hRq-ei0U. Then use the questions above to discuss the story.

4. APPLY 10-12 minutes

Summarize the story, emphasizing the covenant between two friends and the concrete ways that they (especially Jonathan) lived out their commitment to each other. Say, *These acts of friendship and consistency helped David trust Jonathan with his own life—even though that meant Jonathan would have to betray his father. That's a lot of trust. How do you get someone to trust you that much?* (allow responses). *The old saying goes, "The only way to have a friend is to be one." How does that relate to trust in friendships?* (allow responses).

Distribute copies of the handout sheet and pencils and give everyone 5 minutes to fill out the three sections of the trust quiz, working alone. Stress honesty; answers won't be shared.

When everyone is finished, ask: *What does trust have to do with parents? What does trust have to do with God?* Now ask them to use the back of their sheets to make three lists with the headings:

- PEOPLE I TRUST WITH MY LIFE
- PEOPLE WHO TRUST ME WITH THEIR LIVES
- THINGS I CAN DO TO BUILD TRUST WITH MY FRIENDS

Give them 3 minutes. Ask if anyone would like to share ideas from the third list.

5. RESPOND 7-9 minutes

True Friends Can Be Trusted. Ask everyone to *write a message* (on paper or use a favorite social media venue) to one of their friends that includes a covenant of trust; they are to tell that friend how they want to be trustworthy in the future. Have everyone find a place to be alone, either in the room or spilling into other places, if they're available. Give them 4 minutes. Participants may choose individually whether or not to send the message.

Close in group prayer, asking for God's help when trusting and being trustworthy gets tough.

LOOK AHEAD

For **Session 2**, contact four volunteers to participate in the **Oprah Meets Orpah** talk show (see Explore the Bible).

INSIGHTS FROM SCRIPTURE

They were unlikely friends. Jonathan was the son of the first king of Israel, and David was just a shepherd boy, the youngest of a common family in Bethlehem. But, with David's dramatic introduction into Saul's royal court, they met and bonded in a friendship for life.

According to 1 Samuel 18:3, Jonathan made a covenant with David, because *he loved him as his own soul*. This voluntary covenant, made in the presence of the Lord, was regarded the same as a blood relationship. They pledged themselves to each other; they knit together their souls. Jonathan sealed the covenant with the gift of his armor, robe, and weapons. While a common way to seal a new relationship, it was nonetheless a weighty gesture on the part of a prince.

» THE COVENANT IS TESTED

David and Jonathan's friendship was tested, however, by the jealousy and insecurity of Jonathan's father, Saul. As 1 Samuel 18:12 describes it, "Saul was afraid of David, because the Lord was with him but had departed from Saul." David, the poor shepherd boy, was successful in everything he undertook, and was winning the hearts of Israel away from the king. That infuriated Saul.

Saul's threats on David's life (19:1; 18:11; 19:10; 18:25) drove David to seek out his friend Jonathan. Yet Jonathan had already defended David to his father once (19:1-5), and was in a sticky situation himself. Would Jonathan side with father or his friend?

David won out. Jonathan swore allegiance to him, whatever the cost or outcome. And so David, fully trusting Jonathan, laid out a plan to test whether or not David was safe at the royal court.

The plan was sealed with a renewal of the covenant (20:12-17). Both young men had much to lose in this situation. David wanted reassurance that he would be warned if Saul plotted against him. Jonathan, on the other hand, knew that if open conflict erupted between Saul and David, he could lose any claim to the throne. In such a case, he wished David well (20:13). He asked that if he survived such a battle, the covenant would still be remembered, even if they fought on different sides. He was especially concerned for his children. The two walked away, realizing that the covenant they made could cost them their very lives.

» WHEN A MORAL MAN CANNOT BE KING

From Saul's point of view, he was doing Jonathan a favor. He could see that as long as David lived, Jonathan would never become king. He was desperate to preserve his royal line. But Jonathan, perhaps sensing that God had already chosen David to be the next king, would not ascend the throne at David's expense. He, unlike Saul, was able to appreciate greatness without feeling inferior.

If Jonathan lacked the leadership skills to be king, he well made up for it in moral character. It was he who initiated the covenant, and he who upheld it at the risk of losing everything. Jonathan sacrificed his entire future for his friend, because he was trustworthy in everything he said he would do. True friends can be trusted. So David placed his very life in Jonathan's hands.

On the morning they enacted their plan with the arrows, David and Jonathan had to part, not knowing if they would see each other again. Though it was life-threatening for both young men to be seen together, David ran to Jonathan when the messenger boy was gone. He bowed three times, and acknowledged the good services done him by his friend. But it was more than that. Jonathan had risked his own life to save him. No wonder he "wept the more" (20:41). In this touching final scene, the two friends pledged kindness and faithfulness to each other and to their families "from generation to generation." It was a promise they both would keep.

Exploring tough questions facing youth today

"WHAT? Of course my friends TRUST me! I'll do anything for 'em!"
"WHAT? My PARENTS? Can they TRUST me? Honestly? WELL...."
"WHAT? GOD? Do I trust God? Can God trust ME? Hey, this is getting a little personal, isn't it?"

FILL OUT THE FOLLOWING QUIZ, honestly, AND GET SOME ANSWERS!

My Friends

1	2	3	4	5	6	7	8	9	10
I don't think about building trust									I work to build trust
1	2	3	4	5	6	7	8	9	10
It's hard not to talk									I keep all secrets
1	2	3	4	5	6	7	8	9	10
I tell them what they want to hear									They know I'm brutally honest
1	2	3	4	5	6	7	8	9	10
I'm careful about what I lend									I share my possessions
1	2	3	4	5	6	7	8	9	10
I freak when someone is more talented than I am						Someone's success doesn't mean I'm inferior			
1	2	3	4	5	6	7	8	9	10
I risk my life for no one									I would risk my life for my best friend
1	2	3	4	5	6	7	8	9	10
I take credit when it's due me									I honor my friends before myself

Parents

1	2	3	4	5	6	7	8	9	10
I fudge on house rules									I keep house rules
1	2	3	4	5	6	7	8	9	10
My life is my business				I'm totally honest with my parents about what's happening in my life					
1	2	3	4	5	6	7	8	9	10
My parents are in outer space									I try to listen to my parents

God

1	2	3	4	5	6	7	8	9	10
I'm in control of my life									I trust God to be in control
1	2	3	4	5	6	7	8	9	10
I do my own thing							I try hard to hear what God is telling me		

How to Be a True Friend : Session 1

Permission is granted to photocopy this handout for use with this session.

>>> **SESSION 2**

TRUE FRIENDS ARE LOYAL >>>

>> KEY VERSE

But Ruth said, "Do not press me to leave you or to turn back from following you! Where you go, I will go; Where you lodge, I will lodge; your people shall be my people, and your God my God." (Ruth 1:16)

>> FAITH STORY

Ruth 1:1-18

>> FAITH FOCUS

Naomi and her family moved from Bethlehem to Moab because of a famine. Her husband died there, and her two sons married Moabite women, Ruth and Orpah. Then her sons died, leaving all three women widows. When the famine was over, Naomi set out to return to Bethlehem. Ruth and Orpah followed, and Naomi begged them to turn back, for their own sakes. Orpah returned, but Ruth, out of loyalty to Naomi, remained.

>> SESSION GOAL

Encourage participants to be loyal friends in their relationships while maintaining their loyalty to God.

>> Materials needed and advance preparation

- Copies of the handout sheet for Session 2
- Pencils/pens
- Newsprint/marker or chalkboard/chalk
- Bibles
- Prepare four volunteers for the **Oprah Meets Orpah** talk show (*Option A* in Explore the Bible)

TEACHING PLAN

1. FOCUS 3-5 minutes

Ask: *Have you ever tried to buy friendship?* You probably won't get any yes answers, but you'll have their attention. Distribute copies of the handout sheet and pencils as you explain the rules to "Buy a Friend": *Each one of you will have $25 to buy the ideal friend. Look over the different categories and how much they cost, and choose wisely. You have 2 minutes.* Call the group back together when the time is up and ask for sample "friends" they bought.

2. CONNECT 4-6 minutes

Say, *We can't really buy our friends, but we can choose the kind of friends we want to have and be.* Then have them list the top ten things a true friend should have or be. (Other ways to ask the question: *What do you really value in a friend? How do you know when you have a true friend?*)

Put their ideas on newsprint or chalkboard and prioritize those qualities together as a group. Do it in a countdown style if you want. ("The number 10 quality that makes a true friend...") If the group does not mention loyalty as a quality or value that they like in friends, then ask them what they think about loyalty in friendship.

3. EXPLORE THE BIBLE 13-16 minutes

Shift to this activity by saying: *Loyalty is an important quality in real friendship. The Bible tells the story of a woman who was even more loyal than her own friend thought she ought to be.*

Read Ruth 1:1-18 together, using volunteer readers. Then choose one of the following options:

>> **Option A:** Set up a talk show, **Oprah Meets Orpah**, where Ruth, Naomi, and Orpah are guests of a talk show host like Oprah Winfrey (who says her name, incidentally, is a misspelling of Orpah). You will have prepped your "guests" in advance with some background information (see Insights from Scripture). You as leader can be the interviewer, like "Oprah," or give the part to someone who can swing well with the role. The rest of the group is the audience, with the opportunity to raise their own questions as the interviewer circulates among them. Here are some starter questions:

- *Orpah, would you do it the same way again?*
- *What kind of financial troubles were you in, Naomi?*
- *What does it mean for a woman of your time period to lose her husband and sons?*
- *Ruth, what are some things you gave up by going with Naomi?*
- *Ruth, wouldn't it have been more respectful for you to obey Naomi, rather than be so stubborn about going with her?*
- *Naomi, why do you think Ruth insisted on going with you?*
- *So, how did things work out for the three of you women?*

The interviewer may not want to use all these questions immediately, allowing the audience to ask similar questions. Don't let the talk show drag on; when you think that the group has begun to experience some of the emotions and hard decisions that these women must have felt, have the interviewer thank the guests and take a commercial break. As you wait to come back "on the air," ask for questions or comments from the rest of the group. Say, *Can you imagine giving up your home, and probably your only chance at a secure life to help someone?*

>> **Option B: Fan fiction** is writing that remixes characters, places, or plots from existing narratives to tell new, original stories. If there are people in your group who enjoy writing and imagining, invite them to generate ideas (using online fan fiction sites for help) of how they might expand the story of Naomi, Ruth, and Orpah, or take the characters in a completely new direction. Have the creative writers explain why they went the way they did.

4. APPLY 12-15 minutes

Use the following scenarios to get the group thinking about what loyalty might mean in different situations.

1. Your friend has gotten involved with the wrong crowd. He's doing drugs. You've talked to him about it, and he says he can stop whenever he wants to but he doesn't. His grades are suffering, he's stealing money from his parents to buy the drugs, and he's not acting like himself anymore. He's begging you not to tell anyone about it but some adults have started to ask you about the changes he's undergone. **What does loyalty mean?**

>>
"God sends us friends to be our firm support in the whirlpool of struggle. In the company of friends we will find strength to attain our sublime ideal."

St. Maximilian Kolbe

2. Your best friend was just diagnosed with an eating disorder. You know other students and classmates are making comments about her changed physical appearance and eating behavior. She wants you to walk with her to classes and eat with her, but that means enduring stares and whispers behind your back. **What does loyalty mean?**

3. Your good friend from church has become very vocal about supporting the death penalty, as a high profile case has been in the news. The church has long been opposed to capital punishment, and you personally believe very strongly that it is wrong. Other kids are beginning to tune him out, and he keeps calling you to do things together. **What does loyalty mean?**

When discussion winds down, or after 15 minutes, have the interviewer/talk show host sign off. Then debrief with these questions: *Could you relate to any of those situations? If not, why not? What do you think Jesus would have done in those situations?*

5. RESPOND 10-12 minutes

Covenant together to do one or more of the following, or make up your own:

- Eat the same food at the same time each day for a week (they don't have to get together).
- Pray for the group for one minute at the same time each day for a week.
- Set up an electronic message board with regular times to send and receive messages of friendship and support.

Close in prayer, asking God to help you to be loyal friends and faithful disciples.

LOOK AHEAD

Find a short rope or bungee cord (2-4 feet/1 meter long) for next session.

INSIGHTS FROM SCRIPTURE

Naomi was a woman in dire straits. She was a Hebrew refugee in the pagan land of Moab, having fled a famine in Bethlehem some years before with her husband and two sons. But her husband and sons had died. She was a widow, with no money, and few options for supporting herself. On top of that, she did not even have grandchildren to carry on the family name. She considered this the ultimate disgrace. As she told her daughters-in-law, "No, my daughters, it has been far more bitter for me than for you, because the hand of the Lord has turned against me" (v. 13b). She felt betrayed by a God to whom she had been faithful.

When Naomi decided to return to Bethlehem, her daughters-in-law, who were "good girls," went with her. Their loyalty and love for her was mutual; Naomi wanted them with her. But she also wanted the best for them, and logic argued that the best was not in Bethlehem. First, they would be foreigners. As childless widows, their only hope of security and a life without disgrace was to go back to their family of origin or remarry. That was only a remote possibility if they moved with Naomi. Even the Near Eastern custom that obligated a man to marry his dead brother's wife was in this case moot, since all the men in Naomi's immediate family were dead. There was no way out. Naomi used every argument to remind Ruth and Orpah that there was no chance for a decent life if they followed her to Bethlehem. Continued loyalty to her meant a sacrifice of everything worth living for.

» ORPAH

Orpah listened to the strong and wise argument of her mother-in-law. It was only after this second argument that she turned back to her home. History has painted Orpah as the unloving, self-seeking daughter-in-law, but to her honor, Orpah was acting in obedience to Naomi. Naomi twice insisted that she turn back and gave good reasons. Orpah was responding as a good daughter-in-law should.

» RUTH

But where Orpah was submissively obedient, Ruth was lovingly disobedient. Ruth's response to Orpah's departure and Naomi's plea is one of the most eloquent and best-known statements of personal loyalty and sheer courage. In these words are a gentle insistence, a quiet resolve, and a discernment of the deep loneliness of Naomi and her own duty to stand by her mother-in-law.

With these words, Ruth said three important things. When she said, "Where you go, I will go," she was expressing an appreciation of the joyful responsibility of personal friendship. When she said, "Your people shall be my people," she expressed a willingness to lose her own tribal claim to join a people that would include both of them. With the phrase "and your God my God," she even took on a new religious identity. She expressed a deeper understanding of a universal God than Naomi did when she said that Orpah had gone back to her people and her gods. The common belief of that time was that the gods were "tied" to the land. If one moved, one's god did not necessarily follow along. Ruth was serious about making Naomi's God her God. The word she used for God was *Yahweh*, not Elohim, the common word that foreigners used for God.

» DISASTER TO FULFILLMENT

Naomi's God did become Ruth's God. God blessed Ruth—and Naomi—abundantly for her "loving disobedience." An almost hopeless situation turned into a new marriage for Ruth, financial security for Naomi, and best of all, a grandson named Obed. Through this grandson would come the great King David and, later, the Messiah himself. Ruth, a foreigner with extraordinary loyalty and courage, became part of the most blessed lineage of all.

BUY A FRIEND! BUY A FRIEND! BUY A FRIEND!

In Real Life — Exploring tough questions facing youth today

Today is your lucky day! You have 25 dollars to buy the ideal friend! Spend your money wisely.

2 DOLLARS WILL BUY
___ someone with a car that runs
___ someone athletic
___ someone who lives close
___ someone who has no other friends

3 DOLLARS WILL BUY
___ someone talented
___ someone your age
___ someone who has great video games
___ someone who has a nice car
___ someone with the right clothes

5 DOLLARS WILL BUY
___ someone with the same interests
___ someone who is generous
___ someone who is a good listener
___ someone outgoing

6 DOLLARS WILL BUY
___ a friend who is "all that"
___ someone who is gorgeous/hot
___ a friend with an unlimited supply of money
___ someone very intelligent

10 DOLLARS WILL BUY
___ someone absolutely, totally loyal
___ a dedicated Christian

How to Be a True Friend : Session 2

Permission is granted to photocopy this handout for use with this session.

>>> **SESSION 3**

TRUE FRIENDS TAKE RISKS >>>

>>> KEY VERSE

The Samaritan woman said to him, "How is it that you, a Jew, ask a drink of me, a woman of Samaria?" (Jews do not share things in common with Samaritans.) (John 4:9)

>>> FAITH STORY

John 4:1-26

>>> FAITH FOCUS

Jesus stopped by a well in Samaria. There he asked a Samaritan woman for a drink. This was culturally taboo, because their ethnic groups despised each other and because they were not the same gender. But Jesus, in taking this risk, offered her "living water." She accepted this new abundant life.

>>> SESSION GOAL

Encourage participants to risk forming new friendships and deepening the friendships that they already have.

>>> Materials needed and advance preparation

- Old piece of rope or bungee cord (2-4 feet/ 1 meter long)
- Bibles
- Copies of the handout sheet for Session 3
- Writing paper, pencils/ pens
- Two or three pairs of scissors (optional, see Apply)
- Coffee can and matches (optional, see Apply)

TEACHING PLAN

1. FOCUS 5-7 minutes

Ask people to name the greatest risk they took this past week. Note especially any friendship risks they took. Then ask them to listen as you read two case studies about friendship risks. Their job is to discuss the situations as a group and decide the best action in each case. Your goal in the discussions is not so much to work for consensus, but to bring the risk issues close to home. Use these two case studies or make up some of your own.

A. A new kid at school sits alone in the cafeteria. You don't know what it is, but she just doesn't quite fit the look and style of your group. She doesn't have a bad look or style, just different. She looks a little self-conscious. What do you do?

In Real Life | How to Be a True Friend 21

> "We have inherited a large house, a great 'world house' in which we have to live together—black and white, Easterner and Westerner, Gentile and Jew, Catholic and Protestant, Moslem and Hindu—a family unduly separated in ideas, culture and interest, who, because we can never again live apart, must learn somehow to live with each other in peace."
>
> Martin Luther King, Jr., "The World House"

B. Your parents are struggling in their marriage. Things feel confusing at home, and you angry and a little scared. Someone in your youth group asks how things are going. You know this person well, and you are in a semi-private place. What do you do?

2. CONNECT 4-6 minutes

Change the focus by saying: *We've been talking about imaginary situations and people. What about us? When have you risked the cool factor to sit with someone new? When have you really shared from the heart with a friend?*

Have the participants sit in a big circle. Show them your piece of rope and ask them to pretend it's a bungee cord (if you can get a bungee cord, all the better). Ask them to think of a time when they either befriended a new person or were the new person someone befriended. Share a story of your own first, modeling vulnerability. Keep it short. Then toss the rope to someone in the circle, and ask them to share their story. That person then tosses the rope to someone else until everyone has had a chance to share. Reassure them that they may pass.

3. EXPLORE THE BIBLE 10-13 minutes

Shift to this next activity by saying: *Friendship can be risky, like bungee jumping off a high cliff and hoping the cord doesn't break. Jesus bungee jumped to reach people.*

Take about 30 seconds to summarize the situation between the Jews and Samaritans (see Insights from Scripture) as the participants turn to John 4:1-26. Call for three volunteers to read the passage dramatically; have one person be the woman and one Jesus. Skip the "Jesus said" parts and read the dialogue only. Use a narrator for the other non-dialogue parts. Thank your volunteers and proceed with this explanation and corresponding questions:

1. *Jesus had to overcome a lot of barriers to show acceptance to this woman. The first barrier was* **RACIAL**. *In your opinion, is there racial prejudice in our community today?* (Get responses after each question.) *The Jews hated the Samaritans more than any other group because they were "half-breeds" (originally Jewish in ancestry but then they intermarried with foreigners). Nothing infuriated the Jews more than these "unclean" Samaritans claiming their same beloved ancestors. What group in our society would be hated like that?*

2. *The second barrier had to do with* **GENDER**. *In those days men were not supposed to talk to women in public, not even their wives. Yet Jesus talked not only to a woman, but to a woman possibly shunned by others. The passage tells us she was at the well around noon (the sixth hour). It was proper to go in the early morning or evening. This woman may have been so looked down on that she drew water at midday to avoid seeing the others. What actions mark someone as a loner in our society? For the most part, do you think these loners want to be alone, or do they just feel like outcasts? Do you talk to social outcasts? What do you say?*

3. *The third barrier was* **RELIGIOUS**. *The Jews and Samaritans each had their own temple. The Jews were not to touch anything that a Samaritan had touched—it would make them unclean. Knowing this, what was the real problem behind Jesus asking the woman for a drink? By talking to her as he did (see v. 22), what was Jesus trying to say to her?*

4. *Jesus wasn't the only risk-taker. He asked the woman to risk telling who she really was. What really* **PERSONAL** *questions did Jesus ask her? How do you feel when friends ask you really personal questions? How did the woman respond to Jesus' question? Was it the truth or a lie? Why do you think she suddenly brought up the worship issue in verse 19?*

Summarize by saying, *Did you notice how Jesus gently hangs in there with the woman, not really prodding, but not really letting her off the hook either? He wants to be her friend in the greatest sense of the word; he wants to give her living water—everlasting life. He even takes the risk of telling her he is the Messiah.*

4. APPLY 15-20 minutes

This Apply has two parts:

Part 1: Continue by saying, *Now it's our turn to risk showing our real selves to each other.* Distribute copies of the handout sheet with the interview questions and review the instructions and questions there. Separate into groups of four, separating close friends and cliques if you have any. Instruct them to go around the circle, every person answering question #1, and then everyone answering #2, and so forth. Encourage everyone to participate fully, although they may pass. Remind them to listen carefully, and to pay attention to the meaning behind the words.

Draft as leader the person whose birthday is closest to the date you are using this session; the leader will go first, and be responsible to keep the group on task. Ask every group to pledge confidentiality. As they work, help groups who are stuck or are spending too much time on one question. Allow 8-10 minutes.

Part 2: Listening exercise. Say, *Usually someone will only risk opening themselves to another if they sense a good listener. Jesus was a good listener. He heard not only the Samaritan woman's words, he also listened for the meaning behind her words—her tone of voice, her body language. Let's find out how well you listened to each other in your small groups.*

Distribute writing implements, and have everyone turn their handout sheet over and divide it into quarters, one quarter for each of the four questions. Everyone is to list the names of the people in their small group. Then list beside each name how they remember that person answering the question at the top of that quarter of paper. They can include a guess about how the person was feeling when they answered (nervous, eager, whether or not they were really risking). Allow 3 minutes. The exercise is a self-challenge on how well they listened, and will not be "graded."

Now get rid of the papers so that no one needs to feel self-conscious about having their answers to potentially risky questions in print. Tear up papers into tiny pieces or provide scissors for each person to shred their papers into the wastebasket. Or, if you can go outside, burn them in a can.

5. RESPOND 3-5 minutes

》 **Option A: Risking exercise.** Say, *Like Jesus, we have living water to share. We can give living water to lonely people who need our friendship and to our old friends, who need us to be open with them. Do we dare risk it?* Tell the group that you will be asking them to make a public commitment, which can be risky in itself. During the upcoming prayer, explain that you will ask them to step forward if they are willing to talk to a new person in the coming week. You will ask them to take another step forward if they are willing to be more themselves with their old friends in the coming week. Then gather in a circle for a prayer of commitment. Use your own or use this prayer:

LOOK AHEAD

For next session you will need to make some simulation cards (see Focus). You will also need a friendship ring or bracelet.

If you choose **Option A** of the extender session, use the plan for your next session. If you are using this unit in a weekly Sunday school and choose **Option B**, hosting a retreat, start planning and inviting people now.

Loving God who hears us,
*   we ask for the courage and wisdom to listen well.*
We ask for your strength and love as we risk giving living water to our friends.
We want to step forward as a way of committing ourselves
*   to reaching out to people we don't know. (step forward one step)*
God, we also want to step forward as a way of committing ourselves
*   to sharing intimately with our friends. (step forward)*
Give us courage, God. We can only do it if we walk close to you. Amen.

》 Option B: As a group, name some things that people are *afraid* to risk (telling they are gay, they are [or aren't] a virgin, their parents are splitting up, they aren't sure they believe in God, they're suicidal). Is there a good reason they won't tell about those things? When is it appropriate to confide in someone? Inappropriate? Discuss ways to be a friend even when someone can't or won't reveal everything about themselves. Make sure to include the following ways to be a friend:

- Simply be a listening ear. Your friend may not be looking for solutions, but for someone to listen.
- Ask your friend, "How can I help?" This helps the friend be clear about what they do and don't need from you.
- Know when to get outside help. When the situation is beyond you, offer to help put your friend in contact with an adult you trust or a professional trained to deal with the issue.

Conclude with a prayer asking for God's strength and love to help us risk reaching out to new and old friends, and for courage and wisdom to listen well.

INSIGHTS FROM SCRIPTURE

At first glance, John's account of the Samaritan woman and Jesus might seem like a strange passage for a study on friendship. It is rich with lessons on spirituality, salvation, and evangelism. But focus on the initial encounter, when Jesus approached the woman. That encounter models risks that we also must take to reach out to others and to share our inner selves. The fact that Jesus challenged almost insurmountable obstacles to relate to this woman can inspire us to break down barriers as well.

》 THE RACIAL BARRIER

It is first of all remarkable that Jesus even traveled through Samaria (4:3-4). The typical Jewish traveler to Galilee would have avoided this direct route by traveling through Transjordan to the east, because the Jews hated the Samaritans. Even Jews who showed reasonable tolerance of other races were openly contemptuous of them. These people were half-breeds. Many years ago the king of Assyria brought people from Babylon and other Gentile cities and settled them in the cities of Samaria. These people intermarried with the Jews who also lived there (2 Kings 17:24). Racial purity was so honored by the Jews of Jesus' time that they were infuriated by these half-pagan people who claimed cherished patriarchs like Abraham and Moses as their ancestors. Thus Jesus was doing an unthinkable thing by talking to a Samaritan.

>> THE GENDER BARRIER

But not only was Jesus talking to a Samaritan, but to a woman! That was also a cultural taboo. The rabbis frowned on a man talking with a woman in public, even his own wife! A Jewish commentary on the Torah, Aboth 1:5, reads, "He who talks much with womankind brings evil upon himself and neglects the study of the law and at the last will inherit Gehenna (hell)."

But there was a problem even beyond the fact of her gender. It was customary for women to draw water in the early morning or the cool of the evening, never in the heat of the day. Yet she was at the well at the sixth hour, or about noon, probably to avoid feeling shunned by the other women. She had had five husbands (4:18) and was now living with another man. Even if Jesus had not already known this, her presence at that unusual hour marked her an outsider. And yet, despite these factors, or maybe because of those factors, Jesus came to her.

>> THE RELIGIOUS BARRIER

Religion was another sharp dividing line. The Samaritans built a temple at Mt. Gerazim, near Shechem, according to dictates in Deuteronomy 27:4. Infuriated by a rival temple, the place was demolished by John Hyranus more than a hundred years before Jesus lived. The Samaritans, smoldering about the temple's demise, held their Passover on Mt. Gerazim each year near the ruins. They also resented the later centralization of the sanctuary on Mt. Zion in Jerusalem. On one occasion they retaliated by scattering human bones throughout the temple during a Passover festival. In short, Jews and Samaritans couldn't stand each other.

>> THE ENCOUNTER

It is within this context of hostility that the encounter took place. Jesus even asked her for the wrong thing—a drink of water. It seems a simple and reasonable request, given he was hot and tired from traveling. But in that setting, it was unthinkable, for as John emphasized, "Jews do not share things in common with the Samaritans." This doesn't mean that the two groups never had any direct contact with each other. But Jews would never share the same food vessels with Samaritans for fear of ritual contamination. Yet Jesus, having no cup of his own, was willing to drink from a cup that Samaritan lips had touched.

The woman was shocked that he asked for a drink. But even more shocking was how he already knew her so well—her whole life, failed relationships and all. This shook the woman. This was no ordinary man, but a prophet. To top it all, his offer of "living water" touched something deep inside her. Here was a man who broke through multiple barriers to reach out to her, a man who knew the way to heal her aching heart. Could he be the Messiah?

"I am he, the one who is speaking to you" (v. 26). Not only did Jesus offer her living water, but she could see with her very eyes the source of that water. She ran to the city with the good news. She had found the Messiah. And she found him because Jesus, despite obstacles, found her.

Risky Business

In Real Life — Exploring tough questions facing youth today

The woman at the well was wary of this stranger who risked his reputation to speak to her, and then seemed to know about her life, as well as risked telling her who *he* was. Like the encounter of Jesus and the woman, do we dare show our real selves?

Take turns in your group answering these interview questions. Go around the circle, every person answering question #1, and then everyone answering #2, and so forth. Participate as fully as you can—"pass" if you must. Listen carefully and respectfully to each other. Pledge with each other that what you say will remain confidential.

The person whose birthday is closest to this date is leader, and will go first, and be responsible to keep the group on task. You have 8-10 minutes. The questions are:

1. What is your nickname? How did you come by it?
2. What is your secret goal or ambition?
3. What is one thing you wish everyone knew about you but you haven't been sure how to tell them?
4. What is your greatest fear?

How to Be a True Friend : Session 3

Permission is granted to photocopy this handout for use with this session.

>>> **SESSION 4**

TRUE FRIENDS FIGHT >>>

>>> KEY VERSE

The disagreement became so sharp that they parted company. (Acts 15:39a)

>>> FAITH STORY

Acts 4:36-37; 9:19-28; 11:21-24; 15:36-40; 2 Timothy 4:9-11

>>> FAITH FOCUS

Barnabas and Paul were two key players in the growth of the early church. Barnabas sponsored Paul when he was a new Christian, when other believers were still suspicious of him. The two were partners in ministry until there was a sharp disagreement over Mark, who had earlier deserted them. Paul and Barnabas parted ways, but later reconciled, and Mark was able to travel with Paul again.

>>> SESSION GOAL

Encourage participants to expect conflict and to pledge not to walk away from it in their relationships.

>>> Materials needed and advance preparation

- Plan for a simulation by making cards and choosing a situation (see Focus)
- Sticky notes or quarter sheets of scrap paper, writing implements
- Copies of the handout sheet for Session 4
- Bibles
- Chalkboard/chalk or newsprint/markers
- Friendship ring or bracelet

TEACHING PLAN

1. FOCUS 6-9 minutes

Before the session, decide upon a potentially volatile decision for the group to make. Choose your own situation or use this one—ask the group to choose between two fun events they could do in the future. In addition, put one of the following sentences on each of six index cards:

- You're in a bad mood. Whatever the group decides, you're against it.
- You're very concerned that everyone's opinion is heard.
- You work for peace.
- You hate wasting time making decisions.
- You're wishy-washy; you hate to make waves.
- You fly off the handle easily when things don't go your way.

At the start of the session, pass these cards to the first six people to arrive; if your group is small, reduce the number of cards. Whisper to these people that they are to obey the cards during the ensuing discussion. When everyone has arrived, announce that they have a decision to make, and watch the simulation unfold. After 5 minutes, call the group together and explain the simulation. Debrief by asking each cardholder their feelings, and then asking the others how they felt.

2. CONNECT 3-5 minutes

Now ask the group about conflict in their own lives with an impromptu quiz. Distribute sticky notes or quarter sheets of scrap paper, and instruct them to number 1 through 4. Assure them their answers will be anonymous and confidential, and then have them fill in their answers as you ask:

1. How many times do you fight with your friends in one week?
2. How many times do you fight with your friends in one month?
3. How many times have you broken up with your best friend?
4. How many close friends do you have?

> "A quarrel between friends, when made up, adds a new tie to friendship."
>
> St. Francis de Sales

Gather the papers, and during the small group time in the next activity, figure the averages by adding together all the numbers for each question, and dividing by the number of papers. Announce the averages at the end of the session.

3. EXPLORE THE BIBLE 10-12 minutes

Shift to this activity by saying: *As our quiz will probably show, everyone (or just about everyone) fights with their friends at one point or another. It really gets tricky when more people get involved, with one stuck in the middle...*

Divide into three groups, distribute copies of the handout sheet, and go over the instructions there, as well as assign each group one of the scripture clusters at the top of the handout. Draft a recorder for each group (the person in the group who is wearing the most red) to write the group's answer to this question: **WHAT KIND OF GUY IS BARNABAS?** Explain that in this Bible story, not everything is spelled out explicitly, so reading between the lines and making a few assumptions is acceptable.

Gather the groups back to report their answers. Then, as a whole group, read 2 Timothy 4:9-11. Ask: *What must have happened between Paul and Mark? How was Barnabas in a small way responsible for this? How do you think Barnabas' loyalty to Paul made Mark feel?*

4. APPLY 15-18 minutes

Say: *Barnabas and Paul were two friends who fought but also worked things out. God wants the same for us.*

Now proceed to the bottom of the handout sheet ("And...Action!"). Again, assign each group one of the starter sentences with accompanying scripture. They are to read the sentence(s) and scripture aloud to the entire group, and then perform a skit to illustrate the response the Bible passage calls for. Allow 7 minutes for working up the skits.

Take turns presenting the skits. Affirm each group for their efforts and debrief with questions like, *Does this ever happen in real life? What would you do? What would Jesus do in this situation?*

5. RESPOND 7-9 minutes

Instruct the group to follow up on the principles learned from the skits and make some **conflict conduct rules**. Write down ideas as they brainstorm, then condense them into five principles that can be written on newsprint or a chalkboard. Use the scripture references from the handout sheet for help. Make a group commitment to these rules by passing around a friendship ring or bracelet. As the ring or bracelet gets passed around, have each person commit to the conflict rules. If someone wants to pass, they will at least have to explain why.

As a lead-in to the closing prayer, announce the results of your informal quiz (see Connect above). How much do your group members fight with their friends? Then close in prayer, asking not that all fighting cease, but that Jesus, the great Mediator, help you transform conflict in friendships.

LOOK AHEAD

The footwashing observance at the end of the next session requires one basin and towel for every 6-8 participants. Plan this event carefully to make it worshipful.

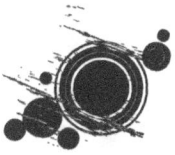

INSIGHTS FROM SCRIPTURE

There are three reasons to study the character of Barnabas as a model of friendship.

- **First**, Barnabas exemplified at least three characteristics of a great friend. He was generous, committed, and loyal.
- **Second**, he ran into interpersonal conflict. It's important to realize that conflict happens, so the Bible is full of conflict descriptions.
- **Third**, the conflict got resolved. Luke does not give much detail, but we can deduce from other scriptures that Paul, Barnabas, and Mark were able to work out their differences and continue their common ministry.

>> BARNABAS

(Acts 4:36-37; 11:21-24)

Barnabas, a.k.a. Joseph, was generous. He sold a field and gave the money to the apostles, because he supported the believers' practice of communal sharing. No one claimed private ownership of any possessions. What radicals! But this was necessary to help believers put spiritual and community realities first. The result was that no one in the community was in serious need.

So the story depicts Barnabas as generous and faithful to God, trustworthy, reliable, and loving to people different from himself. In fact, the apostles named him Barnabas as a compliment; it means "son of encouragement" in Aramaic. Surely God was working through Barnabas! Enter Saul/Paul...

>> IT PAYS TO GET IN WITH THE RIGHT GUY

Saul had experienced a major "aha" moment on the road to Damascus. Dramatic as Saul's (who then became known as Paul) conversion was, the persecutions he had led still weighed heavily against him with the disciples in Jerusalem. Barnabas got the job of convincing them of the reality of Paul's conversion. But he risked being arrested by Paul and, worse, being rejected by the other disciples. But with the well-known Barnabas speaking on his behalf, the disciples accepted and welcomed Paul.

›› SPONSORSHIP BECAME FRIENDSHIP

(Acts 13:13; 15:36-40)

Paul and Barnabas were together for some time, working well as a team along with other companions. Then Barnabas' cousin, John Mark, left the team to return to Jerusalem (Acts 13:13; Col. 4:10). It was a bigger problem than it first seemed and brought Barnabas and Paul into sharp contention (Acts 15:36-40). When Paul suggested returning to the churches in Galatia, Barnabas wanted to give Mark another chance and take him along. But Paul struck back with a firm no. Maybe Paul was still angry over Mark's defection. Perhaps there had been theological confrontation like Paul and Peter had (Gal. 2:11-21), or even some leadership rivalry (Acts 14:12). Whatever had happened, Barnabas was caught in the middle, having to make hard choices in the conflict between Paul and his cousin. He took Mark with him to Cyprus, and Paul headed the other direction.

›› DID TIME DO THE HEALING?

(2 Timothy 4:9-11)

Approximately four years passed. Paul was in prison in Rome, writing this letter to Timothy, giving final instruction and encouragement to the one who would carry the torch after his death. In his closing comments, he wrote of specific people working with him in ministry. Of particular note was Demas, another man who had deserted him. He also mentioned Mark. But this time, there was no accusation. He asked Timothy to bring Mark to him, for he "is useful in my ministry" (v. 11).

What happened in between? The scriptures do not give us a full picture, but we may assume that Paul and Mark were reconciled. How much credit goes to Barnabas for this development, we can't know. But surely the vote of confidence he gave Mark was an important factor in both Paul and Mark's lives. It seems likely that Barnabas and Paul were also reconciled. Barnabas, the "son of encouragement," was committed to his friends and to transforming conflict in a positive way.

Exploring tough questions facing youth today

Just about everyone fights with their friends at one point or another. It really gets tricky when three or more people get involved, with one stuck in the middle…

In your group, identify someone (person wearing the most red) to write your group's answer to this question: **WHAT KIND OF GUY IS BARNABAS?** In this story, not everything is spelled out explicitly, so reading between the lines and making a few assumptions is acceptable.

You will have one of these scripture clusters to help you answer the question:

- Acts 4:36-37; 11:21-24

- Acts 9:19-28

- Acts 15:36-40

Report your answers when the whole group gathers again. Then read 2 Timothy 4:9-11.

- *What must have happened between Paul and Mark?*
- *How was Barnabas in a small way responsible for this?*
- *How do you think Barnabas' loyalty to Paul made Mark feel?*

AND... ACTION!

You have 7 minutes to take your beginning sentence(s), along with the assigned scripture, and develop and **perform a skit** to illustrate the response the Bible passage calls for. As you present your skit, read the sentence(s) and scripture aloud to the entire group.

- "Getting even...that would be the ticket!" Matthew 5:38-42.
- "Can you believe what she did? That was so stupid. I'm heading over to straighten her out." Matthew 7:1-5.
- "That idiot had no right to say what he said about me!" Matthew 18:15-17.
- "If he doesn't get elected club president, I'm outta here!" 1 Corinthians 1:10-13.
- "She broke the rule, so she'll have to live with the consequences...." Galatians 6:1-5.
- "No way, I'm not telling her why I'm mad. She knows what she did." Ephesians 4:25-27.

Take turns presenting the skits, and then discuss: *Does this ever happen in real life? What would you do? What would Jesus do in this situation?*

Permission is granted to photocopy this handout for use with this session.

>>> **SESSION 5**

TRUE FRIENDS SERVE EACH OTHER >>>

>> KEY VERSE

[Jesus said,] "So if I, your Lord and Teacher, have washed your feet, you also ought to wash one another's feet." (John 13:14)

>> FAITH STORY

John 13:1-17

>> FAITH FOCUS

It was their last supper together. Jesus, knowing his death was approaching, wanted to show his love for his friends and to help them with one more lesson on humble servanthood. He washed their feet, the most menial job of a slave. Peter couldn't bear the thought of his teacher doing this, but Jesus convinced him of his need for this gift. Afterward, Jesus told his disciples to follow his example of service.

>> SESSION GOAL

Encourage participants to show their love for each other through giving and receiving service.

>> Materials needed and advance preparation

- Prize for winner of the "Greatest in the Group" contest (*Option A* in Focus)
- Bibles
- Copies of the handout sheet for Session 5
- Timer or watch
- Basins and towels for footwashing (one basin per 6-8 participants), warm water

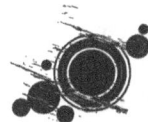 

TEACHING PLAN

1. FOCUS 7-9 minutes

>> **Option A: Greatness contest.** Compete for the title of "Greatest in the Group." Each person has 1 minute to prepare and 30 seconds to perform an act of greatness. You as leader will be final judge. *Do not* divulge Jesus' standard of greatness, which is humble servanthood. Suggestions for greatness feats: a good joke, musical performance, a feat of strength, persuasive speech called "Why I Am the Greatest." Expect everyone to do something, even the shy ones, but don't push it. Give title and prize to the one whose idea of greatness came closest to servanthood. If no one comes close, consider offering the prize to someone who has shown some kind of service anytime so far in the session. Or don't award the prize at all!

>> **Option B:** Prove your love. Give participants up to 5 minutes to come up with a way to show you that they love you (the leader). They may work individually, in small groups, or as a whole. They may use props they find in the room, the church, or outside. **Restrictions:** They may not use writing or words.

After everyone has had a chance to "show their love," express your thanks and care for them.

2. CONNECT 3-5 minutes

Ask: *What's the most loving thing you ever did for one of your friends? Your friend did for you?*

3. EXPLORE THE BIBLE 8-10 minutes

Shift to this activity by saying: *Being really great or really loving is different things to different people. Jesus' definition was: "The greatest one is the one who serves" and "I love you so much I will serve you." But that was hard for some of the disciples to hear....*

Direct the group to Luke 13:1-17. Assign volunteers the parts of Jesus, Peter, and the narrator. In this dramatic reading, the characters read their spoken words, and the narrator reads everything else. No one reads the "Jesus said" and "Peter said" parts.

Give a one-minute mini-lecture on footwashing in Jesus' day: who did it and why, when it was done, how the job was viewed (see Insights from Scripture). Next, call for ideas of how this story would look today. What would be the awful menial task Jesus might do for the people in your group? For example, would Jesus offer to clean out their room, pick up the dog poop or clean the cat's litter box, do their homework for them? Brainstorm for 30 seconds or so.

What might Peter have said when Jesus did this modern-day equivalent of footwashing? Talk it out and then act it out (if your group is so inclined).

4. APPLY 16-18 minutes

Break into groups of four so that people can share in a less threatening setting. Make sure there are no more than four in a group, and that groups have enough space to talk without being heard. If you have access to other rooms or space outside, use it. Stress group participation and confidentiality. Distribute copies of the handout sheet. Each person answers each question, going all around the circle for question #1, then #2, etc. Assure them, though, that it is always okay to pass. Assign the person wearing the most earrings (if no one has an earring, the person with the most finger rings) to lead. The leader begins each question and keeps the group on task. Set the timer, allowing 15 minutes. Give five and one-minute warnings before wrap-up.

5. RESPOND 10-13 minutes

>> **Option A:** Say, *Jesus tells us we should wash each other's feet just as he washed the feet of his disciples. So that's what we will do. It might seem vulnerable, embarrassing or humbling, but there's something special that happens to us as we serve each other in this way.*

Instruct the group in how to do a ritual footwashing. You may want to follow the ritual performed on Holy Thursday at your parish. Otherwise, follow this procedure:

Separate genders into two circles if this will reduce any tension. Otherwise, have the whole group sit in a circle and explain the procedure. Have everyone take off shoes and socks.

>>

> **"When you forget yourself and think of others, this is love! And with the washing of the feet the Lord teaches us to be servants, and above all, servants as He was a servant to us, for every one of us."**
>
> Pope Francis

Begin by kneeling down before the person on your right and washing one foot at a time. This need not be a thorough washing, just a gentle wetting and drying of each foot. After you have dried both feet, both of you stand up and hug each other. You might want to say "Peace be with you" or choose not to say anything. Then this person kneels down before the person on his or her right and so on.

Your feet (the leader's) will be washed last. After your feet have been washed, call for a group hug and close in prayer.

>> **Option B:** Choose another symbol of service to each other, akin to washing feet, and follow the same procedure as for the footwashing, substituting your own symbol. This could be washing of each other's hands, massaging feet, or choosing one of the tasks the group came up with in Explore, above.

LOOK AHEAD

For **Session 6**, gather symbols of commitment (see Focus), and prepare three pieces of newsprint (see Connect). Prepare two people for the Explore the Bible interview.

Also, if you chose the extender option of doing a retreat to solidify relationships in your group, finish planning for it.

INSIGHTS FROM SCRIPTURE

What does it mean to be a servant? John passionately illustrates Jesus' servanthood and sacrifice, played out in a scene of footwashing. There we see how Jesus' life is a model for our servanthood, and that we are servants because he, our Lord, was a servant. We can learn Peter's lesson of receiving as a necessary part of belonging to Christ. And we can begin to understand how servanthood is the way to a fulfilling life.

>> JESUS, THE ULTIMATE EXAMPLE

As Jesus and his disciples sat down for the last meal they would eat together, he knew that his execution was at hand. He could have chosen other ways to demonstrate his love for them, but he chose instead to do a chore that not even Jewish slaves were required to perform (slaves of other nationalities did it). He did it in the context of profound disappointment in one of his friends, Judas. He did it in the context of the upcoming Passover, a celebration of deliverance from slavery. He did it knowing he did not have to do what he was about to do (v. 3). He did it in the context of immense love for those sitting with him. He chose to wash their feet.

>> RECEIVING AS WELL AS GIVING

Peter watched closely this unprecedented behavior. Maybe he was feeling guilty because he had not offered to do the task himself before supper, at the appropriate time. In the custom of that time, when people visited the home of a friend, the host welcomed them by seeing that their feet, dusty or muddy from the road, were washed. It was a degrading task, usually performed by a slave, but it was not unheard of for someone who was *not* a servant to wash feet as a way of showing devotion. Wives sometimes washed the feet of their husbands, and children the feet of their parents. As a disciple, Peter might have performed this service for his teacher. So by the time Jesus reached him, Peter couldn't take it anymore. He rejected the paradox of a slave-king; he did not understand what Jesus was doing.

This exchange between Peter and Jesus carries a lesson about friendship. Part of being a friend and a servant is being able to receive help as well as to give it. Peter was too proud to accept Jesus' act of servanthood. Many people today would rather help their friends than accept help. But to push away another's service is to shut the door to an intimate friendship.

›› WE ARE TO DO AS HE DID

The "Teacher and Lord" (vs. 13) willingly washed the disciples' feet, reversing the "natural" relationship of rabbi and disciple. If it was possible to bridge such a gap, it should have been easier for disciples to wash each other's feet. Jesus informed them that if they showed each other the humble love symbolized by footwashing, they would be blessed. So what is proper for Jesus, the Lord, is proper for us. "I have set you an example..." (v. 15). If we don't know what our values should be, if our priorities get confused, if we flounder for a better way to be a friend, we only need to look at the perfect Friend. He shows the way.

We have been called, or sent (v. 16), to be servants. It is not optional. By the footwashing, Jesus showed what he had come to the world to do, foreshadowed his humiliating death, and gave a glimpse of his future glory. He showed his followers the way to abundant life. If we follow that way in our friendships, we will be blessed.

Exploring tough questions facing youth today

Jesus showed his love to his disciples by washing their FEET. We don't usually wash each other's feet (will they stink, are they ugly, are the nails ragged?), but Jesus does call us to LOVE and SERVE each other in the same radical way he did.

In your small group, answer these questions. Be HONEST! That's part of loving and serving each other. Everybody does question #1, then everybody does question #2, and so on. Find out about TRUE SERVANTHOOD.

1. If Jesus were to "wash your feet" today, what would it be like?
    a. He would cleanse me from_____.
    b. He would say, "Don't be afraid; trust me."
    c. He would give me the desire to follow his Way.
    d. He would help me realize that he loves me no matter what.
    e. _____

2. If you were to "wash the feet" of your friends, what would it look like?
    a. I would let them have their way and take a back seat sometimes.
    b. I would rejoice in their accomplishments.
    c. I would share my true feelings about our relationship.
    d. I would help them through a difficult time.
    e. I would share my needs and let them help me for once.
    f. _____

3. Part of servanthood is the receiving as well as the giving. Peter (in John 13:1-17) had a hard time with that. Are you willing to let your friends serve you? Why is it so hard?
    a. It's too embarrassing.
    b. It makes me feel humble.
    c. I don't want to admit that I have needs.
    d. I don't have needs.
    e. It's not okay to have needs in our group
    f. _____

4. Jesus said, "Now that I, your Lord and Teacher, have washed your feet, you also should wash one another's feet. I have set you an example, that you should do as I have done for you." How does Jesus expect us to follow his example?

5. Jesus says that we will be happy or blessed if we serve one another. Tell about one time when you served someone, and how it felt.

6. Take turns praying for each person in your group as you each answer this question: *How can this group serve me through prayer?*

Permission is granted to photocopy this handout for use with this session.

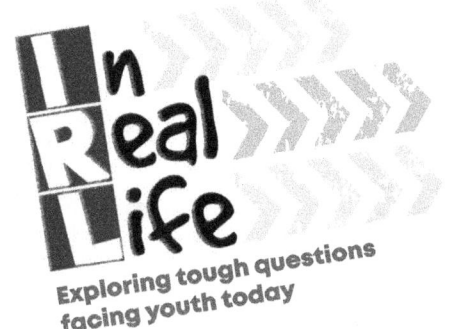

>>> SESSION 6

TRUE FRIENDS COMMIT THEIR LIVES >>>

>> KEY VERSE

"No one has greater love than this, to lay down one's life for one's friends." (John 15:13)

>> FAITH STORY

John 15:9-17

>> FAITH FOCUS

Jesus taught that abiding in him and loving other people are closely connected. When one abides in Christ, as a branch is connected to the vine, one has the ability to love others. Jesus gave us the example of this love by laying down his life for us, his friends. When we abide in him, and commit
to loving one another, we will be better at friendship, and will have joy.

>> SESSION GOAL

Encourage participants to commit their lives to their community of friends through the power of abiding in Christ.

TEACHING PLAN

1. FOCUS 3-5 minutes

>> **Optional:** Before the session, gather things that symbolize commitment in our society such as rings, contracts, letter jacket (commitment to a team), baptismal records, etc. Scatter these throughout the room.

When participants arrive, ask them to make a commitment to do one of the following for the next three minutes (time it):

- *stand on one foot (no holding on to anything)*
- *rub someone's hand*
- *sit on a chair (without the chair), with back against the wall (hard on the quads!)*
- *hug someone*

>> Materials needed and advance preparation

- Symbols of commitment (optional, see Focus)
- Timer
- Chalkboard/chalk or newsprint/markers
- Three pieces of newsprint, five feet long, titled MONEY, TIME, and EFFORT.
- Pens, pencils, markers
- Bibles
- Prepare two people for the Explore the Bible interview
- Copies of the handout sheet (prepare one with answers to the interview—see sidebar in Insights) for Session 6

In Real Life | How to Be a True Friend   39

Two catches: Each person must try to fulfill their commitment in the same three minutes. For example, a person sitting on a "chair" cannot be hugged by someone else, though someone standing on one foot *can* conceivably be hugged. **PLUS**, the group must brainstorm answers to the following question at the same time they are doing their "stunt":

What are some typical commitments people make in their lifetime?

Write ideas on the chalkboard or newsprint as they brainstorm. After 3 minutes, put an end to the stunt "commitments." If you scattered commitment symbols in the room, ask participants if these symbols hold any meaning for them.

2. CONNECT 7-8 minutes

Now ask, *To whom or to what are **you** committed?* Direct them to the newsprint posters entitled MONEY, TIME, and EFFORT, and hand out markers. On the MONEY paper, they should list the top three most expensive things they bought last year, **OR** the largest amount of money spent on one shopping trip. On the TIME poster, they should list the top three things to which they devote their time (besides sleep). On the EFFORT sheet, they should list the top three things into which they put the most effort. They do not need to sign their lists. After 5 minutes, have everyone sit down. Read at random some lists off each poster and comment on their commitments.

3. EXPLORE THE BIBLE 13-16 minutes

Shift to this activity by saying: *We've been talking about commitment. Jesus made the ultimate commitment—laying down his life—to show us the greatest friendship. Where could we get that kind of committed love?*

Have a volunteer read John 15:9-17, and invite the rest of the group to listen for Jesus' definition of love and true friendship. Ask for those definitions after the reading. Distribute copies of the handout sheet and give these instructions: *Thinking of Jesus as someone who really wants to be your friend, fill out this imaginary interview. Write what you think Jesus would have said to the interviewer. Use the scripture passage to help you.*

Give the group 5-8 minutes to fill out interview sheets. Watch for any who seem stuck. Give a one-minute warning when time is almost up.

Then have your interviewer, Chris Chen, ask "Jesus" the interview questions. "Jesus" may use the copy of the handout sheet with the Bible verse "answers" (see Insights from Scripture). After all the questions have been asked, allow the audience to share their responses, especially those that may be different from the way "Jesus" responded.

>> TRUE FRIENDS:

- can be trusted
- are loyal
- take risks
- fight
- serve each other
- commit their lives

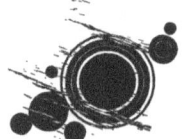

4. APPLY 15-20 minutes

Talk to the participants about Jesus' total commitment to them. Remind them that they are to love one another with the same kind of love. Love like that has at least six key ingredients, outlined in this study. Introduce the idea that they are ingredients of *agape* love, love that is spiritual, not sexual, in its nature. Contrast that to romantic or sexual love, *eros*.

Have the group list the six key ingredients in true friendship outlined in this unit's study (see side-bar). Have everyone turn over their handouts and record the six characteristics as they are mentioned, **OR** choose to depict each of the six characteristics on their Facebook (or favorite social media) page.

Then invite them to find a place alone (in the corners of the room, outside, elsewhere in the building) to:
- sit QUIETLY and evaluate the quality of their top three friendships according to the six characteristics.
- consider what they are willing to do to put any missing *agape* characteristics into those friendships.
- find or think of a symbol of one of the characteristics that is especially significant to them.

Have people pledge to return within 10 minutes, or round people up after that time.

5. RESPOND 8-10 minutes

》 Option A: Gather together again, but break immediately into groups of four (or keep the whole group together). Instruct the group(s) to use their symbol ideas from Apply and decide on **one symbol** that would signify their commitment to each other. If they have trouble, suggest things like a soccer ball with everyone's name on it, a cross that includes something from everyone, hand-decorated T-shirts, a body of Christ sculpture. Give them 5 minutes.

If you have split up, bring the groups together to agree on one symbol. Spend time, if possible, crafting that symbol.

Conduct a circle prayer, with each one praying for the person on their right. If you completed a symbol, pass it to the person praying. Prayers may also be offered silently. This can be a scary experience, but as you model a relaxed attitude and an expectation for participants to pray, they will follow your cues.

》 Option B: Plan a litany of commitment. Write the starter sentence below on newsprint or a chalkboard. Gather into a circle, and explain that the group will recite the starter sentence at the beginning of the litany, and after each person has a chance to share. Anyone who wishes may place a friendship symbol (or tell an idea for a symbol) in the center of the circle. (These symbols are the ones they came up with in Apply.) They should also tell which friendship characteristic it symbolizes. End with the litany sentence, followed by AMEN.

God of love, we commit ourselves to you and to each other, here in this group.

 INSIGHTS FROM SCRIPTURE

John 15 paints a beautiful portrait of friendship. It is a portrait of community and of the willingness to lay down one's life for those in that community. It is to give out of love instead of out of obligation. It is to be chosen by God for the great and difficult gifts of loving.

›› THE TRUE VINE

The disciples were familiar with the motif of vine and branches. Like branches, we need to stay connected to ("in") Jesus, the Vine, to stay alive and produce fruit. If the lifeblood and sustenance are broken off, we wither and die. Self-sufficiency is out. But even the healthy branches are pruned and trimmed to re-channel their energy to be even more fruitful. So we are disciplined to become healthier. And a healthy plant—Vine and branches together—bears fruit.

If we are all branches, acquiring our life from the same Vine, then we are also connected to each other—in community. "This is my commandment, that you love one another as I have loved you" (v. 12). As God loved Jesus, so Jesus loves us, so we love others.

›› THE COMMAND TO LOVE

That love for the community is so important that Jesus *commands* us to do it (vv. 10, 12, 17). If we obey this command, we abide in his love. But the only way we can obey him and bear fruit is by abiding in him (vv. 4-5). Here is a circle of being and doing. We love because we abide. When we abide, he gives us the power to love even the unlovable.

›› FRIENDS WITH BENEFITS

Loving others has rewards. First, we remain in Christ's love (v. 10). Second, Jesus calls us his friends, making known to us everything God made known to him (v. 15). Third, he will answer our prayers (v. 7). This does not mean that we can pray for just anything and will receive it. Those who abide in Jesus ask for nothing that would be against his will.

›› ABIDING

Asking for God's will in our lives is just one way of abiding. The idea of "abiding"—being in Christ and Christ being in us—may sound rather mystical. But abiding in Christ has practical aspects. It is being in contact with Jesus. It is like a weak person who can withstand temptation from wrongdoing only when with a strong person. The weak one abides with the strong person in order to stay on the right track. We are life-linked (Gal. 2:20). We spend time alone with him. We let him set our priorities and help direct our lives. In turn, he gives us the ability to do what he does and to love as he loves. He helps us conquer our weaknesses and obtain the godly qualities that are the fruits of the Spirit. He gives us the love needed to love others, even people who are hard to love.

» FRIENDS, NOT SERVANTS

If we abide in Jesus, we become his friends, not simply his servants (v. 15). What an invitation! Like true friends, Jesus takes us into his confidence, revealing to us his identity, his true self. No mere servant would get such attention. And like a true friend, Jesus does not force his friendship; we can voluntarily choose to love him and to be disciples.

But while true friends treat each other as equals, they *still serve one another* (see Session 5). For them such service is not duty but love. If we really love our friends, we should treat them as equals, not as our servants. Instead, we serve them *as equals*. We do not become their servants, only *as* a servant. We must balance the power and share our intimate selves with them, as Jesus did with us.

» FRIENDS OF THE KING

This friendship has special meaning in the context of the Eastern kings. Each king had a very select group of people he had chosen to be "friends of the king." At all times they had access to the king. They could even go into his bedroom in the early morning hours. He shared everything with them, and they, in return, were his closest companions. This is the offer Jesus makes to us.

Like the king, Jesus chooses us; we don't choose him. But it is not a choosing that binds us. It is a choosing that frees us to bear fruit, to really love others, to really be his friends. And all of these things can bring us immense joy (v. 11). As we abide in him, there is joy and love enough that we can give it to others. Through his power, we can love others as he loves us.

» "ANSWERS" TO HANDOUT SHEET INTERVIEW:

1. vv. 12-13

2. vv. 7, 10, 14

3. vv. 4-5; Gal. 5:22

4. vv. 4, 5, 7

5. vv. 5, 10

6. vv. 14, 11, 17

LIVE FROM JERUSALEM: An Interview with Jesus

In Real Life — Exploring tough questions facing youth today

Ever wonder what Jesus would say on the subject of love, friendship, and commitment? We're here live with Chris Chen, reporter for *In Real Life News*, to do just that—get HIS definition on LOVE, COMMITMENT, and FRIENDSHIP.

But Jesus is delayed, still working out things in the upper room with the disciples. We need you to fill out these interview questions as you believe Jesus would respond. Use John 15:1-17 as your guide.

1. **Chris Chen:** You've just heard people on the street talking about the pros and cons of commitment. We now turn to Jesus, who says he has a new perspective on commitment, love, and friendship. Jesus, let's cut to the chase. What's the secret of commitment?

   Jesus:

2. **Chris:** That's a tall order, to lay down your life for someone. What happens to us when we obey your command?

   Jesus:

3. **Chris:** You also call us to, and I quote, "bear fruit." Is this some kind of garden reference or something? What do you mean by this?

   Jesus:

4. **Chris:** So bearing fruit is joy, peace, love. We do all that by *abiding* in you? What exactly does *that* mean?

   Jesus:

5. **Chris:** Are you saying, "Remain in me and I'll give you the kind of love it takes to make a true commitment to people"? How do we know if we're doing it right? How do we know if we've really got commitment?

   Jesus:

6. **Chris:** But if we're doing all this just because you command it, some of us are likely to rebel at the idea of being told what to do. What do you say?

   Jesus:

Chris: So what goes around comes around, heh? To find commitment in friendship, we have to commit ourselves to abiding, resting, in you. Then you'll provide the love we need to follow through on that commitment. Sort of like "to make a friend you have to be a friend." Simple, but tough. Different. And loving. But that's your way, isn't it? Thanks for coming. Jesus Christ, ladies and gentlemen.

How to Be a True Friend : Session 6

Permission is granted to photocopy this handout for use with this session.

>>> EXTENDER SESSION

>> **Option A:** If you choose this option, use it following **Session 3** of the unit.

>> **SESSION GOAL**

Introduce or hone listening skills that are essential to effective communication between friends.

Effective communication has these elements: good listening skills, sincere caring, and a commitment to keep communication going until the message is clear. These are also essential ingredients
in a healthy friendship.

1. Listening test

Introduce the group to the following six ways to improve listening skills*:

- **Give the appearance of listening:** Look interested. Don't tap a pencil or gaze out the window.
- **Use your eyes:** Sixty percent of communication is nonverbal (gestures, body language). Tone of voice makes up another 33 percent. Actual words make up only 7 percent.
- **Learn to concentrate:** Even though you can think up to five times faster than someone can speak, challenge yourself to stay with the person speaking.
- **Avoid interrupting:** Unless someone has gone on for too long, interrupt only to clarify, not to change the focus.
- **Clarify messages:** What you hear is not necessarily what the other person said or meant to say. Reflect back what you heard and ask, "Did I get that right?"
- **Give others time to talk:** Choose words that are few and full.

Then have the group practice doing these things while answering self-revealing questions. Before the session, make up four cards, each with a self-disclosing question on it. (Choose from the list of questions below or make up your own.) Divide into four groups; give each group a card. Everyone in the group must answer the questions on the card and then trade for another card until each group has answered all four cards.

Questions:

- Which of the following restrictions could you best tolerate: leaving the country permanently, or never leaving the state or province in which you now live?
- If you knew that in one year you would die suddenly, would you change anything about the way you are now living?
- You discover your wonderful one-year-old child is, because of a mix-up at the hospital, not yours. Would you want to exchange the child or try to correct the mistake?
- What would constitute the "perfect evening" for you?
- What is your most treasured memory?

>> **Materials needed and advance preparation**

- Prepare four cards with questions chosen from #1, Option A
- Construction paper, glue, and other sheets of paper (see #2, Option A)
- Pens, pencils, markers
- Empty glass bottle (see #3, Option A)
- Bibles

> "It is impossible for us to love other people unless we listen. We simply cannot love without learning to listen."
>
> Martin Luther King, Jr., "The World House"

*Listening skills outline adapted from *One Anothering: Biblical Building Blocks for Small Groups,* by Richard C. Meyer.

2. Lines of communication

This exercise helps people think about their relationships and quality of communication. Give everyone one sheet of construction paper, glue, a pencil, and a sheet of paper. First they are to cut from construction paper a shape that represents them. Then they make a design that represents the group to them. They glue both the design and their shape on the paper, in symbolic relation and distance to each other. Finally, they draw lines representing communication between the two:

- _____ represents regular, genuine communication.
- --------------------------- represents occasional genuine communication.
- ///////////////////////// means talk, but little genuine communication.
- .... means communication through another person (which should be illustrated on paper).

Ask everyone to share their creations and how communication can be improved.

3. Spin the compliment

Play this version of Spin the Bottle as an affirmation exercise. All the same rules apply, except the spinner lays not a smooch but a compliment on the person toward whom the bottle points.

4. Scripture

End with a discussion of Matthew 13:10-16.

>> **Option B:** If you choose this option, use it following **Session 6** of the unit.

>> ## SESSION GOAL

Help participants strengthen their friendships in the group by spending extended time together and intentionally sharing their lives.

1. Plan an overnight retreat at a nearby but private setting. Make sure it has plenty of space and is comfortable.
2. Give the participants time to plan for the weekend event. Invite them during Session 3. Have ready food assignments (everyone helps cook) and a list of things to bring.
3. Start the evening with physical games and icebreakers.
4. After they're tired, switch to a more mellow atmosphere for sharing.
5. Then have a small group session. Divide into small groups of 4-7. If possible, have an adult in each group. Have ready a Bible study or board game with questions that facilitate sharing lives with each other.
6. Call the groups back together again for a worship time. Have another small group and worship time if you are staying over a Sunday morning.

Some suggestions for Bible passages that work well for building community.

- **Luke 12:13-21: The Rich Fool.** Ask: *Where are your riches? How would you like to be remembered? What are three priorities for your life now?*
- **Luke 7:36-50: Jesus Anointed by a Sinful Woman.** Ask: *Who was the person who believed in you before you believed in yourself?*

In Real Life
Exploring tough questions facing youth today

CLUELESS AND CALLED
Discipleship and the Gospel of Mark

What does it take to be a disciple? This study of the Gospel of Mark focuses on the requirements for following Jesus' way and the abundant life that is ours as a result. (5 sessions)

DO MIRACLES HAPPEN?
Signs and Wonders in the Gospel of John

The greatest miracle, recorded in John 1:14 and 3:16, is the miracle of God's love that became flesh and lived among us. But John also included examples of what we more traditionally think of as miracles: the wonder of abundance from little; healing; signs of impossibility and faith; and the resurrection. (5 sessions)

DO THE RIGHT THING
Ethics Shaped by Faith

How do you know what's right and what's wrong? Even when you figure it out, the right thing is often the unpopular or unpleasant choice. This unit offers participants a clearer sense of what it means to claim a faith identity, a foundation that can help them sort out the gritty details of ethics shaped by faith. (6 sessions)

FIGHT RIGHT
A Christian Approach to Conflict Resolution

This unit will help youth understand conflict and its function. They will learn how they can be honest and loving, and explore how conflict can be used for positive results. They will also learn ways to enhance their communication skills. 1 Corinthians. (5 sessions)

GOD IS A WARRIOR?
Violence in the Bible

The Bible challenges us to be reconciled to one another and work for justice. So what do we do with the stories that seem to condone violence or even encourage it? A discussion of issues in the Old and New Testaments. (6 sessions)

HOW DO YOU KNOW?
Wisdom in the Bible

Wisdom literature teaches us that we gain knowledge of the world, ourselves, and God through experience and observation. This unit provides practical, hands-on wisdom to help young people avoid life's snares and grow closer to God. Proverbs, Job, Ecclesiastes. (5 sessions)

HOW TO BE A TRUE FRIEND
The Bible Reveals Friendship's Heart

To be a friend takes skill. Help youth discover the secrets of friendship through various stories from the Old and New Testament. (6 sessions)

HOW TO READ THE BIBLE
Building Skills for Bible Study

What kind of book is the Bible? What does this book mean to me? This unit looks at the Bible as revelation, as history, as literature. Selected scripture. (5 sessions)

KEEPING THE GARDEN
A Faith Response to God's Creation

If Christians believe that God made the world, we do not need any more compelling reason to care for it than that God has handed us a treasure to hold and protect. This unit gets beyond trendy environmentalism and challenges youth to see environmental awareness as a religious issue. Genesis. (6 sessions)

MANTRAS, MENORAHS, AND MINARETS
Encountering Other Faiths

How is Christianity different from other faiths? Why do others believe the way they do? This study can give youth a new appreciation for the uniqueness of Jesus. Selected scripture. (5 sessions)

SALT, LIGHT, AND THE GOOD LIFE
The Beatitudes and the Sermon on the Mount

What can youth expect in a life of discipleship? This unit explores the Sermon on the Mount under four main sections: the Beatitudes, Salt and Light, Jesus and the Law, and Heavenly Teachings. Matthew 5. (6 sessions)

A SPECK IN THE UNIVERSE
The Bible on Self-Esteem and Peer Pressure

Discover God's unconditional love and acceptance of all people. This study will show positive ways to have one's life make a difference, and help youth find ways to resist negative peer pressure and turn it into positive action. (6 sessions)

THE RADICAL REIGN
Parables of Jesus

Jesus used parables to reveal what the kingdom of God is like, and how God relates to us. This study highlights how the parables reveal God's reign as radically different from the world we live in, and what that means for the Christian life. (6 sessions)

TESTING THE WATERS
Basic Tenets of Faith

Discover the biblical roots for the central Christian concepts of covenant, community, and baptism. This short course is a way to test the (baptismal) waters of Christianity before diving in, or review the basics for those who already have. (6 sessions)

WHO IS GOD?
Engaging the Mystery

God is beyond human comprehension, yet desires to be known. These sessions focus on the way we get clues about and glimpses of God from the Bible, God's creation, and church tradition. Selected scripture. (5 sessions)